Missing Shaun

Thomas R. Thomas

BAMBOO
DART
PRESS

LOS ANGELES † NEW YORK † LONDON † MELBOURNE

Missing Shaun by Thomas R. Thomas

978-1-947240-55-1   Paperback
978-1-947240-56-8   eBook

First Printing 2022

Cover art by Dennis Callaci

Layout and design by Mark Givens

For information:

Bamboo Dart Press

chapbooks@bamboodartpress.com

Bamboo Dart Press 023

www.pelekinesis.com

www.bamboodartpress.com

www.shrimperrecords.com

031421 11:08 AM
sold the car
empty space
under the tree

Contents

Epistle

022621 6:58 PM

these days
exhaust us
we are worn
to the bone
stare out
through
vacant eyes
long for
human touch
and if we
have lost a
loved one
breathe in
our
loneliness

Monday, February 15, 2021, 12:56 AM. Modern smartphones document everything in our lives. Count down 6 minutes from 12:56. But that is the end. We need to start at the beginning.

At least at the beginning of the end.

Wednesday, February 10, 2021, 1:16 AM -

going to admit him.

I had just dropped him off at the hospital some time after midnight. He had been in pain most of the day, and we had given him some of his Mom's strong pain medicine. I had gone to bed, and his Mom heard him in the kitchen. She asked him if he was OK, and if he wanted to go to the hospital. He said yes quickly.

We drove to the hospital, and every bump in the road hurt him. As I drove down our street I thought that when I drove him home I would make sure I didn't drive down the long way on our bumpy road.

I dropped him off at Emergency at Memorial in Long Beach. There was a tent across the way and after getting his temperature and asking a few questions a nurse walked him to the emergency entrance. I spoke with a nurse at the tent for a few minutes. He told me that Shaun would be there for at least two hours, and that I should go home.

I drove to the In-N-Out and got a cup of coffee. In-N-Out is comfort food. It is just coffee, and I couldn't eat. He sent me the text telling me that they were admitting him while I was driving. I pulled over and texted back to text me if he needed a ride home, fully expecting to give him a ride home in a day or two.

Friday, February 12, 2021, 8:34 AM -

Need a couple more things. Call me before you leave to drop clippers.

Friday, February 12, 2021, 12:37 PM -

did you get your things?

Yes

Awesome

I'm sitting in the parking lot at Cal Poly waiting to get my vaccine.

Yay

Sunday, February 14, 2021, 4:32 PM -

How are you doing? Are you settled into your space? Do you have privacy?

Early that morning we got a call from his doctor, Dr. Hussain, telling us that she had been asking his permission to call us since he was admitted and that he had finally given his permission Sunday. She said that she was admitting him to the ICU, but that she would still visit him. She told us that she had sat with him and talked with him, knowing how serious his condition was and knowing that he could not have family visiting him.

Sunday, February 14, 2021, 6:20 PM -

Privacy yes. Bad CT Scan.

Dr. Hussain called later to tell us that the CT Scan had found a perforation in his abdomen. Before that they had planned to treat the cancer hoping to shrink the cancer since an operation was not safe, but with the perforation they needed to operate, and the doctors had told Shaun that his chances of surviving the operation were not good. Shaun decided to pass on the operation.

Dr. Hussain told me that she was going to try to get permission for me to visit Shaun.

I had a dinner that I needed to pick up from the Italian restaurant, so I drove to Cerritos to pick it up, and on the way back I got the call that I could go see him.

Sunday February 14, 8:15 PM

I arrive home and force down some soup.

Sunday February 14, 8:51 PM

I leave home and drive to the hospital.

I only sat with him for a few minutes. The PICC line they had given him had given him relief from the severe pain he had been experiencing. He gave me his phone and told me the code to get into the phone. He had a list of people he wanted me to contact, and a personal message for Michelle and I. I told Shaun that I loved him, and asked him if he had any regrets. He said he had no regrets.

He said that I could go, and told me to keep the phone. I gave it back and said that he would need it if he wanted to talk to us or his brother. He told me he knew there would be a lot of tears.

The nurse told me that Shaun wanted me to take his belongings home and went back into the room to collect everything that he had.

Sunday February 14, 10:21 PM

I got home, put Shaun's things down on the couch, and went to bed.

Monday, February 15, 2021, 12:56 AM

I get a call from Shaun's nurse in the ICU telling me that he had passed away six minutes before. I told her that I wanted to come and get his phone, so I got in my car and drove to the hospital. I picked his phone up at the desk in the lobby. The guard that was there told me the she had just lost her brother the day before driving home from Las Vegas.

Monday, February 15, 2021, 12:50 AM...

In the thousands of years that fathers have lost sons and sons have lost fathers this is one more in a long span of time, yet this is this time and these are the tears I am crying, and these eyes are still moist with my pain.

Poems

020921

nothing pricks
your heart like
staring at the
face of your
child's mortality

021421

it's the small
decisions—what
meals and portions
we make for
tonight's meal
when you are
missing

021421

is a life
cut short
taken too soon
or had it
completed
a life fulfilled

021421

greatest loneliness
when you can't
sit with the
ones you love
and hold their hand

I don't know how to feel
watching him lying there
waiting around to die

I can't feel
my heart is numb
no more tears

sleep has stolen
away from me
missing

021521 3:01 AM

> my gut is tied
> reaching up to
> steal my breath

021521 3:12 AM

> and I want
> to scream but
> nothing

021521 4:08 AM

> his life is
> stolen from him
> what is a little sleep

021521 4:13 AM

and in the time of
a terrible virus
cancer comes

raging like a lion
and tears him down

021521 4:27 AM

more silent
scream but no
sounds comes

021521 12:04 PM

now I can cry
as soon as I hear
your sister's voice

021521 6:52 PM

> I wonder where
> he is (if (he is)
> in my thoughts)

021621 4:11 AM

> the tense
> keeps changing
> each minute

021621 4:36 PM

> I leave his door
> open to remind me
> he is not here

reluctant
to share the news
to one more

it hurts to
steal their joy

021621 10:59 PM

regret the time lost
or cherish the time
spent with love

021621 11:49 PM

I hear someone
out front—I look
it's not him

021721 12:18 AM

> hopes and dreams
> close your eyes
> your final sleep

021721 7:37 AM

> in these lonely times
> there were three
> now two

021721 1:19 PM

> I wanted Brian
> for my cousin
> Michelle chose Shaun
>
> William was for my uncle
> to keep him in the family

It's not like he's
moved to New York
and doesn't call

passing by the
cemetery he is not
there really

I was saving these shows
so he could watch them the
new episode is hard to watch

021821 8:21 AM

> he would open
> the shades most mornings
> the room is dark

021921 9:26 AM

> sometimes
> the moment
> takes my breath

021921 9:27 AM

> I was saving
> the papers for when he
> would return

021921 12:42 PM

how do I tell
him I've completed
his list

021921 2:07 PM

his memory
and mind was my
reference

022321 9:35 AM

the pain
in my gut is
still there

022421 9:33 AM

he organized
the coffee table
just before

it's already back
to chaos

022621 2:46 PM

the thought to
burden loved ones
grieves me

022621 10:10 PM

he liked orange
chicken, some food
is hard to eat

I don't recall
if I said I love you
at least with words

Now he knows
what happens after
or not

in the
quiet moments
I cry

031421 11:08 AM

        sold the car
        empty space
        under the tree

031421 11:10 AM

        his ashes
        wooden box
        on his desk

032021 3:02 PM

        COVID fears
        did he wait
        to save us

032121 10:17 PM

there is now
a wisp of memory
as I reach for him

032521 9:35 AM

I cry
I will always
cry

Epistle

I'll stop
counting
birthdays
for you
you will always
be thirty-five
and
never be
more

picked up your
death certificate
today
put it next
to your ashes
this
is
hard
to read

The Final Four
is playing
this weekend
I'll miss you
sitting on the
couch with me
as we
casual
watch the game

Mom misses
you too
especially when
you helped her
but more
when you
could talk
when she
would ask
you questions
about movies
politics and such

it's shameful
I know
but I cry
for you
when I hear
love songs

watching Rent
again
you didn't like
it when
everyone in
High School
liked it because
it was cool
for the moment
and that every
musical sounded
like every musical

remember when we
saw Miss Saigon
The mother of the girl
who played the boy
sat next to us
told us how she
and her husband had
been with the show
for twenty years
she was a choreographer
now and she apologized
that the copter didn't work
it's still my favorite
Musical and now will
always be ours

I loved being your
soccer coach
you were still
not ready to
be too serious
about the game
but you tried to
defend the goal
though you sometimes
ran the wrong way
and your best game
was in the rain
with your jacket
under your shirt
your red hood on
you played your best
game that day and you
got to run in the rain

I can never
say goodbye
the mist
of your memory
is always
in the air
yet
tomorrow you
will not be here
again
so
just for practice
goodbye

I am alone
in my thoughts
alone
touching the fringe
of the ones
I love
in the warmth
of the embrace
of their hearts

twelve thousand nine hundred
seventy seven days
eleven hours, fifteen minutes
how many seconds
over one billion lived
in thirty five years
is it one billion
seconds lost or
one billion lived
did your cup
end half full
or all filled
I have always
told you
I don't believe
in regret
so you closed
your eyes
breathed your

last breath
at the end
of a
full
life

inside the cage
my mind
the walls
turned inside out
where freedom
lives
twisted with this
desire to live
within
without
yet desire
inclusion

your cat
he's decided
it's my job
now to feed him
he harasses me
when his bowl
is empty
he's getting pudgy
in the middle

I think of you
when I close the blinds
I would have never
thought to turn
the blinds up so
they can't look down
and see the computer
in my office I just
don't think that way

you asked me
for a comb
and nail clippers
your phone charger
and your notebook
for your game
you had hope
at least for a
few days

still don't
like some of
the comics you read
I figure the
rare good days
aren't worth
the pain of
reading the
bad strips
I think of you

when I read the
good comics
and want to share
the good strips
I turn
and
you're not
there

there are times
when your
memory fades
I'm sorry
time thins
yet you
are
there
still

what is the
meaning
of death
what is the
use of life and
then we die
what is the
purpose
of death
what do
we
achieve
tell me
what is
the use
of
your
death

I miss you
as the temper
to the storms

I'm sorry
no service
for you yet
we live
in strange
times

as I write
these poems
I remember
you would
be the one
to read
my scribbles
you were glad
I wrote the date

just today I
mourn the death
of a star
as I watch it
blink out
long gone
before we
wrote our
first words

fatherhood is
a thankless job
and when it comes
it is a mystery
I'm still surprised
You said I was
a cool dad

my stomach
is tight too
often
now
warm and
making me aware
always that
I miss
you

I bought a
bag of those
little chocolate donuts

I learned to
freeze them from
an apartment manager
and passed that
on to you—I miss
you more now

About the Author

Thomas R. Thomas lives in Long Beach, CA, and publishes the small press Arroyo Seco Press. Publications include Carnival, Chiron Review, and Silver Birch Press. His books are *Scorpio, Five Lines, Climbing Eternity, in which the world is turned upside down, the art of invisibility, Star Chasing, The High Cost of Dying, three on a wire, Lambs to the Slaughter,* and *Schrödinger's Cat.*

BAMBOO DART PRESS

112 N. Harvard Ave. #65
Claremont, CA 91711

chapbooks@bamboodartpress.com

www.bamboodartpress.com